The Fate of Humanity in Verse

To Mike Perkovich,

We'll always have USC

The Fate of Humanity in Verse

Frank Rogaczewski

American Letters & Commentary, Inc.

ISBN 10: 0982564708
ISBN 13: 978-0-9825647-0-7

Published by
American Letters & Commentary, Inc.
PO Box # 830365
San Antonio, TX 78283

www.amletters.org

This is a work of fiction. Any similarities to real people
or events are unintentional and are for purposes of
illustration. Any similarities to pesuedo-people (aka
"pod people") are inevitable given the cultural milieu
in which the author lives and writes.

American Letters & Commentary, Inc, is a not-for-
profit corporation under section 501(c)(3) of the
United States Internal Revenue Code.

Cover Image: *Teagan at Four* ©2005 by Trey Downey
Book Design: David Ray Vance

for
Beverly

Contents

Working Like a Demon

To combat Karl Marx's forecasts of capitalism's impending doom, mid-20th century science and technology deployed its forces ambidextrously: hula hoops and bikinis on the one hand and the line between labor and leisure on the other. Quicker than you could say, "It's Howdy Doody time," Fifties' sociologists were sent out in droves to drone on about how by the 21st century the workweek will have decreased by eighteen to thirty hours, and how technology will transmogrify work into something almost as pleasurable as the three-martini dinner cruise, the office itself into the home away from your suburban home—without the wife peeking into the rec room, if you get our drift. Robbie the Robot and his android companions will handle the heavy lifting; the clones will do all the second guessing. Got a special project around the house? Make way for the mutants (that's pronounced so that the last syllable rhymes with *ants*). In the future, where we will all wind up at some future date, people will enjoy lengthy vacations and many more paid holidays—not only Thanksgiving, Christmas, New Year's, Memorial Day, Fourth of July, Labor Day, and Columbus Day, but probably a day each for all the other explorers too—Ponce De León Day, Hernando De Soto Day, Leif Eriksson Day, Henry Hudson Day, Zebulon Pike Day, Robert de La Salle Day, Amerigo Vespucci Day, Lewis and Clark Day (or maybe one holiday for Meriwether Lewis and a separate one for William Clark). Our television sets will also be our tanning lamps, advertisements will constantly remind us of the godzillion choices that we have the god-given freedom to make, and thanks to advancements in medical technology, taxation will feel utterly non-invasive. In the future, where some future day will find you, we'll be able to super-biggie-size everything from our French fries and motor vehicles to our soft drinks and unmentionables. Telephones will come equipped with vision screens so that we can see the party to whom you're speaking. Pretty soon you'll be able to see why this poem could be titled "A Visit From Nostradamus." You know, the author of one thousand prophetic quatrains grouped by the hundred and titled "centuries," quatrains written under the influence of nutmeg and best understood in retrospect, being non-chronological, multi-lingual, and riddled with esoteric metaphors and anagrams and all. He clearly had a lot of time on his hands. But he's made some real humdingers of predictions. Conspiracy buffs refer to him as "the grassy knoll-it-all." He predicted Louis Pasteur, General Francisco Franco and Adolf Hitler by name. Certainly, those Fifties' sociologists must've felt like Nostradamus, what with their prognostications of future paid holidays for every other US president. Wait! Now they're foreseeing that by the year 2000 the barrier between work and leisure will have eroded to such a degree that Hollywood actors will run for US president. Imagine that: the Humphrey Bogart White House. Actually, there's some debate as to whether Nostradamus predicted Hitler by name since the original lines—"Bestes farouches de fain fleuves tranner/ Plus part du champ encore Hister sera"—have generally been translated as having to do with mad beasts swimming across rivers and most of their army facing off against the aforementioned "Hister," but the debate begins when one translator reads this word as the name of

Der Führer and another reads it as a reference to a geographical area, most likely the Lower Danube. Apologists for the Hitler reading argue that even if "Hister" refers to a geographical area, it's where Hitler was born anyway. The more skeptical sorts argue that in that case Nostradamus may have been referring to the right family but the wrong cousin, Dieter Hitler perhaps. Apologists flock to the Hitler family tree to see if there ever even existed a Dieter Hitler. "Or maybe Hans Hitler," add the skeptics to keep the apologists occupied. "Or Felix." That's when another party ups and notices that The Monkees' late-Sixties' semi-hit song "Look Out, Here Comes Tomorrow" with lyrics apparently concerning a choice between "Mary" with "lips like strawberry pie" and "Sandra" wearing "long hair and pig-tails" not only foretells the fall of the Twin Towers but narrates in esoteric metaphor the sequence of the attacks. As a result, the Fifties' sociologists decide they would rather be compared to the Delphic Oracle, the source of many prophecies in Greek literature, if you recall, especially in matters of political and commercial enterprises, not to mention marital advice. Moreover, Pythia, who gave the responses that a male prophet then interpreted in verse, could prophesy without being high on nutmeg. At most, she chewed a few bay leaves. "That may be," Nostradamus's apologists say, "but our soothsayer is more concerned with the big questions, like war and death and natural disaster." "You call those big questions?" Pythia's promoters ask. "The Delphic Oracle is the last word on all matters of religion." "Oh yeah?" reply the Nostradamians, "Our guy has foretold the coming of three Anti-Christs. And we bet you don't even know what an Anti-Christ is." And the Delphonics are like, "Do so."

"Do Not," reply the nay-sayers. But more than the social scientists, the Fifties' B-movie directors were downright Nostradamian or Delphonically Oracular, depending on your predilection for prediction. In *our* future the labor problem will be solved with the reanimation of the recently dead (that would be "Labor Plan 9," officially endorsed by the International Monetary Fund, the World Trade Organization, and the increasingly Republican National Labor Relations Board). Vampira wins the "Employee of the Month" award. For the share holders, an end to unsightly demands for wage increases. Just listen to a zombified Tor Johnson: "Me no like economic democracy." For the working stiffs, it'll be the total domination of dead labor over living labor. There will be one national holiday, but only for your boss, whom you will address as "Master." As in, "Me no need health care, Master." Wait a minute! In the future, where, futuristically speaking, we will all someday find ourselves, the multinational corporations will think, "Why not cut the middle man?" You know, the humanoid aliens in the spaceship aiming the reanimation ray at your local cemetery. "We went to the South for cheap labor, overseas for cheaper labor, then for the ultimate low in labor costs, why not Satan's own industrial park?" Think of the perks: free heating! no real overhead! no infernal union organizations! an eternity between coffee breaks! we never knew so many people could be so all fired up to get to work! And you know what else this means, don't you? If you've ever turned to a co-worker and complained, "This is Hell," you were predicting the future.

The Tell-Tale Raccoon

Here's one to make the hairs stand up on the back of your neck: each January 19 since 1949 a mysterious hooded figure arrives by night at the tombstone of Edgar Allan Poe and places there three roses and a half-empty bottle of Martel cognac, leaves these gifts, that is, after raising a solitary toast to that most melancholy craftsman of "Annabelle Lee" and "The Raven." The roses are believed intended to honor not only the poet/critic but also his mother-in-law, Maria Clemm, and his wife, Virginia, who rest nearby in the Baltimore cemetery. The cognac is left for Poe himself, who collapsed in a tavern and died at the age of forty—and here's one to give you goose bumps—one hundred years before the first appearance of the mysterious black clothed and hooded figure at the famous author's graveside. For many decades persons in the know presumed that alcoholism and drug addiction felled the author of "The Masque of the Red Death" and "The Fall of the House of Usher," but in recent years an alternate theory has suggested that rabies may've undone him. With the recent resurgence in rabies deaths in the US—three, four, and five per year due to bites inflicted most frequently by rabid bats, skunks, or raccoons—it would be wise to take the fate of Poe as instructive, even though we don't know for certain that hydrophobia was the cause of Poe's demise or if indeed an afflicted bat, skunk, or raccoon was the agent through which said virus had been delivered and not, for instance, a neighborhood cat or dog, seeing as how we are concerned here with a time previous to the discovery of the rabies vaccine and the prophylaxis practiced upon subsequent generations of canine and feline companions. However, the culprit could very well have been a raccoon, since the animals are opportunists, and, though found primarily along streams and lakes in wooded locales, they may also inhabit urban, residential, and recreational areas, which adaptability garnered numerous American Indian tales for the raccoon of craft, wiliness, and ability to outwit enemies. And while it is in no way suggested that the author of "The Black Cat" was an enemy to raccoons, a rabid animal may have misconstrued him as such. Now here's one to send a shiver up your spine, perhaps suggesting to you a cold spot in your home, evidence of supernatural activity (which reminds us that Jackie Gleason personally oversaw the design of his house so that the rooms were without corners in which the spirits could congregate): each year the hooded figure visits the grave of Edgar Allan Poe while somehow eluding dozens of would-be witnesses parked in cars or huddled together near the cemetery gates, almost leading one to wonder whether the toaster of the gothic author is himself a revenant. The likely development of this particular urban legend has been quelled by one Jeff Jerome, curator of the Poe House and Museum, who's informed the local press of his surmise, based on a 1993 note left behind stating, "The torch will be passed," that the identity of the hooded entity is handed down from father to son, demonstrating the old adage, "The acorn doesn't fall far from the tree," and making my skin crawl when I see in my mind's eye the raccoon clinging to side of that tree beneath what could only have been a gibbous moon, the beast's flame-yellow eyes burning through its bandit mask into my very soul as I confronted it, alone on the litter-strewn Michigan campground from which we had unfortunately failed to remove all the after-dinner leftovers and refuse. Oh, that my need to urinate had not awakened me to the sly and crafty chatterings, the omnivorous munchings, and the unpleasant crinklings of aluminum foil unfolding in all too human-like hands, sounds signaling an end to our idyllic mid-September camping trip. But I would've needed to leave the tent in any case, for as soon as I'd awakened from my nightmare of Edgar Allan Poe explaining to me how he'd planned out every jot and tittle of "The Raven" before he'd set his pen to paper, awakened, I say, to find myself in a ten by eight foot tent with Beverly and the dogs and enough corners for the collection of unimaginable quantities of ectoplasm, a breath of fresh air was clearly in order. But then I heard the stealthy sounds and knew who it had to be: *Procyon lotor*, the common raccoon, belonging to the Class *Mammalia*, Order *Carnivora*, Family *Procyonidae*, and Genus *Procyon*. In other words, fur-faced rapscallions who had to be removed from the campsite before the dogs got riled. So up I grabbed the flashlight and out of the tent I leapt. Then I attempted to turn on the flashlight, which did not come equipped with the trusty, old-fashioned on/off switch nor any button on the side or the back that one might readily click. Meanwhile, there were sounds of scampering, chittering, and—I swear—raccoon tittering. Not that this should be taken as a symptom of generalized anxiety disorder or any such psychological inconvenience, but at that moment I wondered why in the world it had occurred to me to dream the author of "The Philosophy of Composition" expressing himself in language such as *jot and tittle*. I understood that *tittle* was a word for the dot above the *i*, and that it was also more broadly used for any diacritical mark; and that *jot* was another word for *iota*, or *i*, the smallest letter in the Greek alphabet, so that sooner or later *iota* came also to mean "an infinitesimal amount." And I knew that the expression *jot and tittle* went back to Matthew 5:18; hence, I wondered if my dream had in an oblique manner pointed me to the Bible because I was about to face danger and had better refer myself to the 23rd Psalm. I also understood that it wasn't until the 11th century that the dot on the *i*—the aforementioned *tittle*—was introduced, to distinguish the double-*i*, which you'll find ending the occasional Latin plural, from a *u*, but that seemed to be entirely beside the point, and I only mention it here to cross all our *t*'s. I recalled from my dream that Poe had said, "The death of a beautiful woman is the most melancholy topic in the world," but I now remembered that raccoons had been known to carry rabies, that they were in fact the reason that authorities of some states had resorted to the aerial distribution of oral rabies vaccine, that rabies were spread by a bite or a scratch from an infected animal, and that something like seven out of ten American Indian names for raccoons referred to the animal's ability to scratch with its hands, and I opined that the death of myself at the diminutive scratching hands of raccoons would be if not the *most* melancholy topic in the world still pretty sorry. Just then my trembling fingers fumbled somehow appropriately with the flashlight head, and light spilled around the pillaged and plundered campsite, revealing butter or barbecue sauce-slathered aluminum foil, corncobs, potato skins, dog biscuits, watermelon rinds, pretzels, used paper plates, empty baggies and crumpled beer cans. I knew they could scratch with those little hands; I did not know they could crumple beer cans.

Yet the leftover-thieving sneaks themselves were nowhere to be seen. The campsite, while quite a shambles, was raccoon-free. But then I pointed the light upwards, four and a half feet up the tree across the campsite from me, and there he was—bright-eyed and bandit-masked—the leader of the pack and the face of highly-unlikely-but-just-barely-possibly rabies incarnate. Quickly I calculated: if raccoons could spread rabies in a particular direction, let's say west, at about twenty-five miles per year, and Edgar Allan Poe was bitten by a rabid raccoon in the Baltimore area sometime in the autumn or early winter of 1849, that means—and here's one to shiver your timbers—rabies could be everywhere! The raccoon smiled his knowing smile, as if to say, "Go ahead, clean up the campsite. Pick up after me. Just remember this: if against odds of about a million to one you touch something I've salivated upon, and against odds of about a kajillion to one I'm a rabid raccoon, and against odds of a godzillion to one the virus is still active and gets into some break in your skin, you'll be as white and cold as a bust of Pallas in the gray December, if you get my allusion to a poem featuring a certain midnight guest of ebony plumage. But look on the bright side. Maybe your grave will be visited by a mysterious figure too. Y'know, Poe toaster visits a poetaster?" "Oh, yeah?" I replied, "Well, the various American Indian tribes may've had all kinds of different names for you, but I call you *varmint*." Then my flashlight went out again. Afterwards, I thought I should've said, "Pow! Zoom! To the moon, raccoon!" But I doubt it would've mattered. I know when I've been outwitted.

The Man Who Read Marx

Lived in a basement apartment, slept on a fold-out couch in the living room, and longed to look down on the shadow of the clouds on the Rockies. The Alps. "A spectre is haunting Europe," you read in the grammar school library, and *that* was cool, but everything else went over your head. Kind of like *Macbeth*: started with the witches and the incantations and then nothing but domestic squabbles and speechifying. Was he at the Flint sit-down? The women's auxiliary breaking out windows so the strikers inside would suffer less from tear gas. Come all you good workers/ Good news to you I'll tell/ Of how the good old union/ Has come in here to dwell/ In his mind the debate over whether *praxis* included activity *and* thought. One thing though, it meant free creative activity as opposed to—"No one's holding a gun to your head"—laboring as a wage-slave. First manufacturing job, five minutes to lunchtime: you stared at the clock, but the clock had stared at Medusa the assembly line. Called in to clean his apartment after he died, we found stored in boxes that filled the bedroom closet and spilled out into the otherwise empty bedroom copies of pulp science fiction magazines, booklets from a mail-order electronics course, and yellowed stacks of *The Daily Worker*. The shoe factory on the north side and you glued the soles. The paint factory on the near north side and you ran the machine that glued the labels to the cans. The downtrending of manufacturing in the US: 53% of the economy in 1965, 39% by '88, around 12% since 2000. Economists unintentionally let on that capitalism is less than ethical. "Buy low, sell high," they say. Fair

enough with most commodities, but buy labor power low, you sell
humanity short. The place with the rotary turret punch press,

> where the kid got
> his hand busted, and the workers
> stood out in the cold   smoking cigarettes
> and blaming the kid
> or the company

under their breaths. That the history of all hitherto existing society
is the history of class struggle. His old paperbacks and hard covers—
Marx and Engels, W.E.B. DuBois, John Reed, Elizabeth Gurley
Flynn, Antonio Gramsci, V.I. Lenin—from International Publishers.
Was he there for the sit-down? Swept the Klan off the streets of
Fort Wayne and Muncie, shut down the pro-apartheid play *Ipi-
Tombi*. Was he there? Raining down hinges and other fist-sized
auto parts on the police? When the union's inspiration through
the workers' blood shall run/ There can be no power greater
anywhere beneath the sun/ Head down during the McCarthy
era, still the FBI came around and lost him two jobs. The service
sector dominates the economy today. Decline in organized labor:
33% of the workforce in 1945, 24.1% in 1979, 13.9% in 1998....
In his mind, the idea that we are alienated from the process and the
products of our labor, our own creative activity, it follows that we
are alienated from nature, from each other, even from ourselves—

> and you ache for
> the cigarette break
> even though drill press   oil
> soils cigarette paper
> wet filter

alters the fine tobaccos
                the tastes good like
even though whatever's that bright green
                sharp smelling degreasing chemical
adheres to fingers
                smears the square
here and up your nose
                the cool, cool there
                        into your brain

More than soap scum, a brown crust ringed the bathtub. When one of us muttered, "Christ," the landlady apologized, said the man had died of cancer and felt she'd explained, well, everything. How many of us would've loved to say, "You know what a rat-fink is, don't you, Mr. Reagan? A rat-fink is a godforsaken strikebreaker"? The job where you ground the hobs that would grind the gears, that you left in less than a year because you didn't fit in and had to go demonstrate against the Vietnam War and Nixon. Was he there for the Battle of Bulls' Run? A majority of nonunion workers would vote for a union if they could, so that those with representation would be at least 44% today. In your mind he's lying on the cot wishing he could still have a smoke, thinking about how Marx called the working class "a class with radical chains." But—Mother of Christ!—he'd wanted to see the Alps. That capital transforms lifetime into labortime. Oh, deep in my heart/ I do believe/ Visited the Cloisters in Fort Tryon Park, read of monks spending their whole adult lives on tapestries, and had to step out into the garden, take a few deep breaths.

So What Else Is New?

What a difference a
difference makes. My sister's
salt water fish tank becomes
a terrarium. Before you know it
Lotto's been drawn
and somebody
else won. The first time the person
on the street heard of T-cells
they'd already been subverted
into viruses quite
retro and you're just
not the same person anymore
what with cloning and all
three blocks of the street's been
closed off for a mall. The old
gray mare, she ain't what
she used to be a horse
of a different color. Kids hit
puberty before you know it,
before Mr. Rogers
can call it a beautiful day
to retire, quickly as velociraptors
go from lizards to birds or Colonel
Sanders from human to cartoon.
From tooth fairies to insurance

actuaries, everything changes so fast

—taverns to pharmacies to laundromats

to video stores outside of which and

down the block, the occasional

hooker's replaced by a

pamphleteer for the Republican candidate

for state's attorney. The more

things change, the more they

stray the sane. It makes a person

wonder what makes a

                         martini

a martini and not a

Tom Collins. The old mining town

turns into Disney World and you still

got to buy everything at the company

store, just like on campus, where

the only soft drink you can get is Pepsi,

reminding us that Vladimir Lenin

who changed his last

name from Ulyanov, asked

can the proletariat

retain state power?

Well, a little while after that query,

during a heavy snowstorm in the Rockies, a tour bus skidded off

an icy road and took a tumble down a mountainside, flipping over

twice before crashing into a clump of trees. All but one of the

forty-seven passengers sustained injuries later estimated as ranging

from serious to critical—limbs were broken and organs ruptured, people suffered lacerations, concussions, respiratory arrest, muscle tears and abrasions. Making matters worse, the bus had actually been torn open in the fall, and the injured persons had been scattered hither and thither for a few hundred feet down the mountainside. The continuing snowstorm meant that the injured tourists could not count on rescue helicopters in the near future, or for the next couple of days for that matter, and most likely by the time rescuers arrived, the injured would be obscured from view by two or three feet of snow. The tour bus driver scurried hither and thither among the injured passengers and worried, "Oh, whattodo? whattodo?" Luckily, he chanced upon the uninjured man who happened to be a doctor! One Dr. Throckmorton Mahlart. Unluckily, the doctor had recently had his medical license revoked for "unethical practices." Furthermore, the unethical doctor was quite peeved about the action taken by the medical community, and he spat, "The fools! They called me mad!!" Yet the bus driver appealed to Dr. Mahlart's humanitarian conscience, informed him that the bus just happened to be equipped with a first aid kit, and suggested that heroic action here on the mountainside might win the doctor back his license. "Damnitall!" the doctor exclaimed, "I'll do it!" The bus driver sighed with a relief that was tempered only when he continued to hear Mahlart murmur as he administered to the injured, "Mad they called me! Mad! The fools!" And when the helicopters arrived forty-nine hours later, the rescue party beheld a miracle—shock treated, broken limbs splinted, abrasions cleansed and bandaged, open wounds stitched, clamped or cauterized, hypothermia and frostbite treated, tracheotomies performed, ruptured kidneys and spleens repaired, collapsed lungs restored, and three brain and two open-heart surgeries successfully completed. Each and every patient sipped hot cocoa. Holding out his hand to the doctor, the head of the rescue party congratulated him, "You're a hero, my good man. You've saved every one of these people." Smiling, shaking the man's hand, Dr. Mahlart replied, "Not only that, I've changed all the women to men and all the men to women."

Making the Bride

From Pretorius' first entrance to the gothically paradisial nuptial chambers of the newly retired Dr. Frankenstein, once feared dead, now snuggled next to his dear Elizabeth on the dear marriage bed, so glad to be alive, even if only barely, and otherwise quite severely symbolically castrated, and from the first time Dr. Pretorius, out of night and gloom, glances down his long cold nose at his wounded colleague's new bride (who, it will be confessed, failed to greet him heartily), chasing her from the room, you know the outcome will be hysterical, perhaps in the original uterine sense, for it's this reproductive capacity of women that Frankenstein has ever wished to supplant, and this very reproductive organ that he's long envied and vied with, more so than even, say, woman's brain— crucible of intellect and intuition—any covetousness of which Dr. Pretorius has certainly assuaged by growing said organ from seed (his own description of his methods, delineated shortly before Pretorius himself retired to the crypt for wine and cheese with a long- dead "pretty young thing in her own way" and a few forays into the lively art of conversation over victuals with the monster: "food good," "friend," and other such pleasantries, all of which certainly could've been spoken by Bela Lugosi, who by now had decidedly mastered English well enough so that he'd not be required to memorize his lines syllable by syllable, but who, having unfortunately turned down the original, non-speaking monster role due to his infatuation with the Transylvanian vampire and his own wannabe-Freudian theory of women that "it was the embrace of Death their subconscious was yearning for; Death, the final triumphant lover," a theory holding little attraction for film critics of the new millennium, considering its political incorrectness and its apparent disregard for the actual gender construction of the audience—overwhelmingly male—and said audience's obvious allegiance to eros rather than thanatos—given the success of a movie such as *Tremors*, in which Kevin Bacon's character must fend off several aggressive and gigantic phallic worms so that he may learn to appreciate a woman for something besides overly large bosoms—by this choice lived out the end of his days in conditions unbefitting a much-caped man of his post-crepuscular stature, long after resigning himself to roles in skits and sketches on TV variety shows), yet when Frankenstein musters himself from his rest and attends to the affaire du coeur of his creation, it is as if the Muse of mad science herself whispers in his ear, "Physician, heal thyself," for as he fashions the work of his life, the bride to meet the procreative requirements of the monster, borrowing from wherever he will to complete her—the form of her from medical schools and graveyards, the heart of the matter by sending an assistant out to a secluded streetcorner (and in the original script, from Elizabeth herself)—as he notices the now-hysterical townsfolk, who he'd long considered a passel of fools for desiring to stand in his way, are no longer alone in their hysteria—for Elizabeth sees "there!" and "there!" the angel of death, Fritz turns on the monster, the hunters who happen upon the blind man's idyllic cabin site shoot first and ask questions later, the burgomeister hits the road, Minnie shrieks at every opportunity, and even Frankenstein finds himself screaming "She's alive! She's alive!"—he feels physically as though the top of his head were taken off (when in actuality hers has been screwed on), as though he'd called imagination to the help of reason and thereby united truth with pleasure (the monster, smiling wistfully, croaks "Wife!" in a spontaneous overflow of powerful feelings), and he knows the operation such a success that even Bela Lugosi wishes to get on board for the second sequel; then the whole shebang blows up in Frankenstein's face, for, as Dr. Freud tells us, "Sometimes a mad scientist is just a mad scientist."

Whither American Poetry?

Even though there's a perfectly instructive word in the dictionary, *chthonic*, pronounced with the silent *c* and meaning "Pertaining to the gods and spirits of the underworld," fans of Lovecraft have long pronounced the name of the dead god that lies dreaming in his home of R'lyeh *ka-TOO-loo*. Meanwhile, Beverly and I are very happy here in Berwyn. Not that there aren't problems. The mortgage is a bit steep, especially on a poet's salary. And when we walk Sammy, our black lab/border collie mix, some of the neighborhood folks are overly sensitive about his so much as sniffing their lawns. That's right, their lawns, not their gardens, which you might could understand. It's not like their grass is anything to brag about either, has a kind of grayish hue. Have you noticed how both H.P. Lovecraft and T.S. Eliot use initials for their first and middle names? Both men had what you might call marital problems too. Both divorced, although Eliot did re-marry. Oh, and did I tell you about the raccoons? So I'm complaining about the downside of dogwalking to Glynis, who lives nearby but in Oak Park: "I can't believe what pigs people are around here! You can't walk half a block without coming upon broken beer bottles. And all the damn chicken bones..." "Raccoons, Frank," she laughs at my knowledge of nature. "Raccoons get in the garbage cans and pull out the chicken bones." "Hmm, interesting theory," I say. "But how do you explain the beer bottles?" Lovecraft himself weighed in with his own pronunciation of the mad god's name: "The actual sound—as nearly as human organs could imitate it... —may be taken as something like *khlûl'hloo*, with the first syllable pronounced gutturally." Then there's the occasional meteorite to worry about. One bounced off the next door neighbors' garage roof and almost hit one of the four dogs they leave in the yard. As usual, by the next day the space debris had just melted away into the earth, leaving nothing but a spreading gray stain on the grass. Neither Eliot nor Lovecraft have much good to say about sex: it's tedious or gross with the former; with the latter it's out of this world, and I don't mean that in the positive sense. And large bodies of water are inauspicious in both their writings: a watery grave in Eliot, the place from which the fish things spawn to mate with Caucasians in Lovecraft, who was very concerned about miscegenation, which is a word that first appeared in 1864 in a fake abolitionist pamphlet designed to frighten voters away from Lincoln's Republican party. Of course, the town of Berwyn has a long history of—how shall we say?—fear of miscegenation. But that's pretty much in the past: there are a number of Latino families living in Berwyn today, and even a few African Americans. Very few. I dream of a visit to the neighborhood bar, Starry Wisdom Tavern, where dead philosophers and political figures gather to converse and imbibe. Still brushing silphid beetles and dirt from his burial suit, Alexander Stephens complains aloud to any who will hear: "Darby's Prophylactic Pills. That's how I ended my days, hawking some phony nostrum. 'No family should be without them,' that was our slogan. Vice President of the fucking Confederate States of America, and my so-called colleagues and supporters couldn't help me do better. Lee they built a big monument at Richmond. They got Jefferson Davis's name on at least one street and public building in every godforsaken town in the godforsaken South. But me? I 'm peddling placebos 'til the end of my days. Is that any just reward for loyal service and honorable fulfillment of duty?" Meanwhile, Plato picks at a greenish protuberance in his cranium and cajoles Theodor Adorno, "Dialectics are fine, you just don't have to be so negative about them." Before Adorno can answer, I awaken to an insistent scratching at the bedroom window. The neighbors' tree had always leaned toward our house, but now it positively looms at the window before me, branches clawing at the glass as if they'd a mind of their own, hell-bent on breaking and entering. And clinging to a thick gray branch on the neighbors' side of the fence, a family of overly large possum with what look to me like all-too-human faces. I try to calm myself with a "Wimoweh" or two, but instead of "In the jungle, the quiet jungle, the lion sleeps tonight," I find myself singing, "In his house at R'lyeh dead Cthulhu waits dreaming." Notice I pronounce the name *THOO-loo*, because I believe the *c* should be silent. Oh, and did I mention both the poet/critic and the pulp fiction writer were anti-Semitic as all get out? What I'm trying to get at here is this: you've never seen H.P. Lovecraft and T.S. Eliot in the same place at the same time, have you? This knowledge leads us to only one conclusion: Lovecraft's Miskatonic University is none other than Harvard. "Where's the evidence?" you ask. Wasn't Harvard the alma mater to many a Southern plantation owner's son, sent to learn the mysteries of empire and the embarrassment of miscegenation? Wasn't it the home of men of science such as Nathaniel Southgate Shaler, who found the mulatto "peculiarly inflammable material," for "from the white he inherits a refinement unfitting him for all work which has not a certain delicacy about it; from the black a laxity of morals"? And wasn't it the site of famous blatherings-on by Oliver Wendell Holmes, fresh from finding draft resistance and socialist speechifying "clear and present dangers" punishable by long imprisonment? Blatherings such as, "But in the midst of doubt, in the collapse of creeds...the faith is true and adorable which leads a soldier to throw away his life in obedience to a blindly accepted duty, in a cause which he little understands, in a plan of campaign in which he does not see the use"? Now answer me this: If you were an insane dead god who wanted to destroy all of humanity, what dreamier place would there be to begin from? This is *not* good news for a poet. Beverly tells me not to worry, never mind the possum-people staring in the window, go to sleep, but I get up and walk the streets, ignoring the stench of the neighborhood's gray, brittle grass and the raccoon-men tossing beer bottles from their cars, but sick with the thought that almost every significant trend in American poetry since WWII has emanated from Harvard, Cthulhu's home away from home. What was it back in the day? Academic or non-academic poetry? That would be Harvard's Robert Lowell versus Harvard's Charles Olson, Frank O'Hara, and John Ashbery. No wonder Allen Ginsberg was howling! And by the way, did you know that the term *Caucasian* was invented because Mount Caucasus is a hop, skip and a jump from Mount Ararat, where Noah's Ark is supposed to have set down? Get it? Caucasians are supposed to be the new, improved chosen people. A gray squirrel falls from a sycamore and shatters with an odor of drain scum. Great Caesar's Ghost! Even L=A=N=G=U=A=G=E poetry more or less originates at Harvard! Is there no end to the infernal design? And the *c* should be silent not only for the sake of the connection with the word that pertains to gods of the underworld, but also because *ka-TOO-loo* sounds like something you answer with a *gesundheit*. Now that I think about it, the *c* in *Caucasian* should probably be silent too. The remaining *awk* sound of the first syllable would closely relate the supposed racial identity to the word *awkward*, which would disentangle the designation from mythological origins and more firmly tie it to the realistic assessment of these people's dancing. I walk up the alley to my own yard, and, searching for my keys, notice the four dogs next door have all crumbled into gray, stinky powder. I turn myself around, thinking, "Why that low-down, dirty, abysmal, gibbering, gelatinous, cephalopod-headed, cyclopean deity! Even those poets who don't come from Harvard have been trained or influenced by those who do, haven't they?" Past the backyard gardens of overgrown tomatoes, basil and rutabagas that smell like exudate off a real case of gingivitis, down lanes alongside the houses fronted by gray, white and blue American flags, all the while avoiding the occasional noisome meteorite winging by my noggin, all the way to the Starry Wisdom Tavern, where I sit myself down between Julius Caesar and a six-foot raccoon who turns to me and demands, "Aren't you the guy with the dog I saw pissing on my lawn?" On the jukebox the Harvard Alumni Choir chant the return of the Great Cthulhu, but cosmic conspiracy or no cosmic conspiracy, I'm quick to defend Sammy: "Listen, Bud, that's the parkway; it's not your fucking property."

Arse Poetica

I've got this thing about space and place, where atoms are doing nothing but falling straight down. Nothing else happens because there is nothing else—no life, of course, so, on the bright side, no death. Just atoms falling straight down, until one of them— some rebel, some smarty-pants communist—swerves. This is just about where, if you could get them together in the same place at the same time, Lucretius and Heraclitus might agree—if they could understand each other, languages disinclinating themselves from one another and all. Anyway, Lucretius thinks this change (a *clinamen,* he calls it—sounds sexier than it is) causes everything and Heraclitus thinks change *is* everything. We might just jump in at this point and say our world swerves its way into being, atoms of all different kinds of elements compounding and complexicating and then disintegrating back into sub-atomic particles including three flavors of neutrinos—electron, muon, and tau—with the electron neutrinos transforming their flavor as they hurl toward our planet from the sun. Stick out your tongue and you'll see what I mean. Before you can say *clinamen*—actually, it sounds even sexier than I thought—the world is filled with green alligators and long-necked geese, the humpty-backed camels and the chimpanzees, the cats and rats and elephants, and Noah's trying to get them all two by two on the bus before God rides by in his awesome cosmological street sweeper. "Throwing out the riff with the raffwater," God calls it. Fast forward a bit from the days when Heraclitus and Lucretius are hawking their theories on the streets of Greece and Rome, respectively if only semi-respectfully, and you've got William Carlos Williams asking how he can make himself a mirror for this modernity. See, there's a space and a place for everything. But rather than a mirror, I'd like to be a geodesic sphere eighteen meters in diameter containing over 9,500 photomultiplier tubes surrounding an acryllic sphere housing over 1,000 tons of heavy water (that is, water to which a neutron's been added to each hydrogen atom). That's right, I want to make myself a neutrino detector for this postmodernity. We're talking poetics here. Eros is a rose is a sore. Have I got you fired up yet? Well, hold on to your phlogiston, gentlemen; it's going to be a hot time in the old town tonight. For the very idea of everything beginning with atoms simply falling through space until something just happened went out the window a long time ago. Now we've got the Big Bang, and I don't mean that in the defenestrationistical sense of the term, but rather the cosmological. Still, Heraclitus would argue, it's something other than an ignis fatuus to conceive of nature as change. Lucretius would comment that the falling atoms couldn't have gone out the window because space and place were as yet unoccupied by any windows, window frames, or window curtains. Heraclitus would take a deep breath, bring to mind calming images of rusty nails, rotting meat, burning parchments upon which were written *De Rerum Natura*, and launch himself into the old joke (which he never tells the same way twice because he knows everyone's heard this one before) about the elderly woman, who, in need of aspirins, heads out to the shopping mall. A sore is eros is a rose by any other name would smell like feet after having twice stepped in the same old stinky river, heavily polluted in the process of producing photomultiplier tubes. And did you know particle physicists say that protons are not spherical after all but shaped more like sausages or drumsticks or just about anything you cook over a fire? So anyway, the old woman takes the bus to the mall, visits the book store, the grocery, the pharmacy, the container store, and the pet food place. She notices the movie marquee as she passes by, untempted due to the lack of romantic comedies—and I can't say I blame her for swerving away from her choices between this generation's return to the Alamo, the latest filmic meditation on "the Lost Cause," or *Matrix VI*, in which the audience learns that they are watching something that's not real. The old woman—let's call her Clementine—returns to the bus stop, waits and waits, thinking all the time that, in her estimation, the remaining resonance from the Big Bang always smelled like chicken-flavored vegetarian sausages. Lucretius arrives at the bus stop and asks her whether she doesn't think an entirely better explanation is the *clinamen*. She smacks him right upside the head for his use of dirty language, and Lucretius defends himself: "Did I say anything about a cavern in a canyon? Did I so much as mention excavating for a mine?" She smacks him again, this time with her purse, weighted down with fool's gold. The bus arrives and she boards. She sits near the rear, all the while consoling herself from philosophical anxiety by staring out the window, watching the world flitter by—the horizontal version of the original fall. Of matter I mean. Oh, my darling Clementine, then you remember that you forgot what you set out to purchase in the first place. "My aspirins! My aspirins!" And Noah the bus driver, who's heard it all before, shouts back, "I'm behind schedule, lady. You'll just have to hang it out the window." Get it? She hankers after an over-the-counter pharmaceutical and he thinks her butt's on fire. The word changes from the time it leaves her mouth to the time it reaches his ear, just as many words in the language we use have swerved from their earlier incarnations, me wyf. There is no Big Bang in human communication. But wait a minute! That's not a woman; that's old Darryl N. Clementine entertaining the riff-raff by standing up on one of the rear seats and properly positioning himself. And the idea of that flaming derrière hanging out the bus window, veering in and out of traffic, sweeping ever farther from our view: this is the source of poetic vision and insight.

Gratia, Poeta!

Well, that settles it. I looked up her website and there's not one mention of Charisma Carpenter, who plays the role of Cordelia on the TV show *Angel*, being the daughter of John Carpenter (director of *Vampires*, *Ghosts of Mars*, *Prince of Darkness*, the original *Halloween*, and the remake of *The Thing*). This means the greatest father/daughter horror team of all time existed only in my *imagination*, a word for a concept that has pretty much always been with us poets, albeit in a somewhat ambiguous relationship with *fancy*, that being an abbreviation of *fantasy*, from the Latin *phantasia*, itself a transliteration from the Greek, making all these terms more or less kissing-cousins, but I don't want to get all ancient aesthetically philosophical or etymologically medieval on you, so I'll skip right to the part where Michael Anania used to mention in workshops that getting into and out of the poem were two of the most difficult tricks for a poet. Also, he made it clear that you have to earn your O's. In the postmodern world of today the time's long past when the poet can get away with exclaiming all over the poem, let alone apostrophizing this, that, and the other Muse. People just can't suspend disbelief in your transmogrification of an abstraction. When I first signed on as an undergrad, I was like, "Yeats, Yeats, Yeats." I sounded more like a poodle than a poet. Michael Anania and Ralph Mills were kind enough to bring me over to America and plant me a bit more firmly in the 20th century—William Carlos Williams, Ezra Pound, Frank O'Hara, Susan Howe. It's a good thing too. I stopped dreaming of ascending in the ranks of The Hermetic Order of the Golden Dawn—from novice to cloak-holder, I'd fancy—and started thinking more seriously about poetics in the late 20th/ early 21st century, which, of course, reminds us that *Angel* is a spin-off from the TV version of *Buffy the Vampire Slayer*, which stars Sarah Michelle Gellar and apparently is going off the air this spring. The character Angel, played by David Boreanaz on the eponymous TV show, is a vampire cursed with a soul so that he suffers remorse over the evil he has committed and now wants to fight for justice—and also for truth and beauty, I like to think, you know, being a poet and all. In his role as professor of literature, if Michael found you reading *Nova* in class, instead of, "That doesn't go here," it'd be, "You read Chip Delany?" He wouldn't express the same enthusiasm for, say, Stephen King. I'm on my own there. Michael doesn't read anything more graveyardy than the graveyard poets, who were a meditative and melancholy bunch, and guess what was their favorite setting for those meditations—meaning I'm grateful that a poet who could see exactly where any poem wanted to go spent time on my poetry, which always wants to go places like Frankenstein's laboratory, Dracula's crypt, Freddy Krueger's boiler room, Its sewer main, the Dead's shopping mall outside of Pittsburgh, and the Bates' Motel. Named after an Avon perfume, Charisma Carpenter began playing the role of Cordelia, a high school friend of the vampire slayer, on *Buffy* and then graduated to *Angel* with that show's premiere. And though Charisma had only a handful of commercials and a guest appearance on *Baywatch* on her resume, and though Sarah Michelle Gellar has starred in *Scooby-Doo*, won a Blockbuster Award for Best Supporting Actress for her role in *I Know What You Did Last Summer*, and has become a spokesperson for Maybelline, I've always thought Charisma the more interesting actress. Sexier too, especially now that she's impregnated with a demon fetus and positively evil herself. (You would think people would be *negatively* evil, but it never works out that way—some situations simply cry out for an oxymoron.) I guess you could say that for me Sarah Michelle Gellar is like the fancy and Charisma Carpenter the imagination. In the Romantic sense of the terms. You know, where Blake's like, "Imagination is spiritual sensation" and Coleridge is like, "It dissolves...in order to recreate or...to idealize and to unify," comparing the imagination (in a more or less roundabout way) to "the eternal act of creation in the infinite I AM." Where fancy "is no other than a mode of memory emancipated from the order of time and space." Now you can see why John Carpenter should be her father. With his fine sense of the horror film and her presence and acting skill, why, we'd return to a new heyday of horror, one recalling sublime partnerings of previous eras—Elsa Lanchester and James Whale, Janet Leigh and Alfred Hitchcock, Jamie Lee Curtis and John Carpenter. Not that I'm in any way putting down Sarah Michelle Gellar. Even though William Carlos Williams says, "Yes, the imagination, drunk with prohibitions, has destroyed and recreated everything afresh in the likeness of that which it was," the fancy is no slouch either. It may even be—since *imaginatio* came to be used by the Romans as a substitute for *phantasia*—that fancy and imagination are cousins that've been doing more than kissing. Or they are Siamese Twins. And if I were still a member of the Hermetic Order of the Golden Dawn, I'd have to wonder whether there wasn't some cosmic conspiracy at work when *Buffy the Vampire Slayer* goes off the air at the same time Michael Anania retires. Well, there probably is. I mean, how do you thank someone for sharing his knowledge of poets and poetry, his way with line breaks and pentameter. Those of us who've learned from Michael Anania consider ourselves spin-offs from a more critically acclaimed, popular, and longer running TV show. Coleridge's secondary imagination related to the primary imagination, so to speak. Whoa! All these imaginations and fancies in my head! They're making me dizzy and I didn't even take my antihistamine today. And did you ever notice how the pharmaceuticals these days sound like something from the old *Flash Gordon* series? With his pals, Dr. Zyrtek and Dale Allegra, Flash faces the Emperor Ming and the evil Princess Viagra. By the way, I thought I saw Michael Anania on TV, standing next to Mayor Daley at a celebration of Chicago's one hundred and sixty-fifth year, and I thought, "Wouldn't that be something if Michael retired into a whole other career: his own TV show—if not on the WB, perhaps on UPN, in the time slot *Buffy's* left unfilled." It's not unheard of—a poet on TV. Somebody told me he'd seen Charles Bernstein reading a phone book with Jon Lovitz on a Yellow Pages commercial. Can you imagine? Longinus sees in the imagination the source of the sublime when "moved by enthusiasm and passion you seem to see things whereof you speak and place them before the eyes of your hearers." Anyway, it's certainly a show I'd watch, whether Michael played a vampire slayer or a poet/professor. And O! Charisma Carpenter! If you would co-star with him, that would be marvelous!

The Fate of Humanity in Verse

So I'm wending my way through a recent *New Yorker* and what should I read but that the Bush administration's planning another one of their regime changes for nations we just don't like the cut of their jib. This time Iran's the offending countenance. So I'm thinking, "Jeepers! This Seymour Hersh guy is just a bundle of bad news, isn't he?" And then—Holy Oppenheimer!—I come upon this: "One of the military's initial option plans…calls for the use of a bunker buster nuclear weapon, such as the B61-11, against underground nuclear sites." Time was, a poet would come across a disconcerting little factoid like that and it'd be an epigraph to a meditation in verse on lack of compassion and the fate of humanity. So I'm like, "My meditation will be there with bells on." But no sooner am I *in modem meditatio*, so to speak, than the slow-moving, stately rhetorical figures tied to those jingling-jangling bells stumble over the alliteration and collapse under the impossibility of predicting from what angle the -ingling will next arrive. First I think, "Oh, this is a tragedy. I can't even light a little candle of hope in the darkness of our times." But then I'm like, "No, this is a farce." (So sue me, Karl Marx). And really, what's to meditate here? Holy bejeepers! This most Christian of American presidents—and there's Hersh again, with a disturbing quote from an unnamed House member: "The most worrisome thing is that this guy has a messianic vision"—every night when *en déshabillé*, so to speak (Thank God this is not an Imagist poem, kee-rect?), donning his Wild West jammees—some yesteryear's Christmas gift from some shady Saudi Arabian oil tycoon—he kneels and bows his head beside his bed and prays…well, but now you feel kinda like Hamlet, don't you? You look at that *New Yorker* quote again—and, I know, I shoulda set up an epigraph so it'd be easy to find—and you just gotta go with Langston Hughes who wrote of the exploitation of Africans in the Johannesburg mines, "What kind of poem/Would you make out of that?" I know what you're thinking: "Well, he *did* put it in verse." Not to mention, "Langston Hughes *always* had something hopeful to say about dreaming a world and the fate of humankind." But then there's the whole question of what good it'd do anyway. The proletarian poets of the 1930s liked to speak of "art as a weapon," but W.H. Auden, who started out pretty left-wing himself, finally decided that "poetry makes nothing happen," and W.B. Yeats thought politics made "a stone of the heart." And who're you going to believe, a bunch of blacklisted people or the kind of poet who hangs out in anthologies with the likes of William Shakespeare, John Milton, and William Wordsworth? Oh, and that reminds me, this poem isn't anthologized yet, so you don't have an editor to kindly remind you that when the poet exclaimed "Holy Oppenheimer!" he was referring to J. Robert Oppenheimer, the father of the atom bomb, who subsequently suffered McCarthtyite investigation and was stripped of his security clearance for daring to oppose the development of more devastating weapons of mass destruction. All *I* can say is that before and during my career as a professional poet I've held a number of other jobs, including paperboy for the *Chicago American*, gardening helper at the Lincoln Park Conservatory, wall washer and floor stripper at Children's Memorial Hospital, laborer at Tru-test Paints, cashier at Irv's Pharmacy, elevator operator at some unremembered Gold Coast high rise a few doors from The Drake, journalist for a lefty newspaper, laborer at umpteen other sweatshops in Chicago and New York whose names will not be mentioned, hob grinder—and here the anthology editor should probably step in and inform you that hobs are those things from which gears are made—and adjunct college teacher—a job which is sometimes labeled "instructor" and other times "lecturer" but never "professor," if you get my drift; and in not a one of these other travels of travail have I ever wondered whether my particular contribution made an impact. If you water the geraniums, the geraniums grow. Wash the blood down the operating room drains and the tiles are clean. Elevate the rich folks and they will get where they're going. (Whoa! That last sentence works like, "I am one who is acquainted with the night.") Grind the hob and you'll eventually get a gear. Students don't work exactly the same way—at least after high school we don't grind them. But the truth about me is that I'm always second-guessing myself. Clearly, if you light that one little candle and you should stumble in the dark anyways, you'll burn down the damn house. Meanwhile, back here in the *Nuttin Anthology* we're all being told to line up and the editorial staff's deciding how many pages we get. "No Eliot are you it seems to me," the Old Man enunciates at Gwendolyn Brooks. "More's urban than urbane of you. Three pages." Kenneth Fearing's next on the list, but he hasn't shown yet. "No Eliot, that drunken commie bum," the Old Man pronounces. "A page at most, and hold the footnotes too." I go visit the women's caucus, where Edna St. Vincent Millay, Mina Loy, and Angelina Grimké are leading a demonstration bordering on a riot, demanding more pages for women. And here come Margaret Walker and Genevieve Taggard, fully prepared for a sit-in at the preface until their demands are met. By the way, I don't know where that anthology editor was when I told Karl Marx to sue me. He should have reminded you of Marx's famous notion that history repeats itself, "the first time as tragedy, the second as farce." It's an expression I've used repeatedly, whatever that signifies. But now I'm at the rally in the index. And the important names—let me tell you, I could go on and on. Langston Hughes is speaking for Sterling Brown and himself, demanding that their more radical poetry be admitted to the anthology. Muriel Rukeyser and Kenneth Fearing are waiting in line to speak, which might explain the latter's earlier absence. Wait! Here come Ezra Pound and T.S. Eliot dressed in the outfits of the London constabulary. They're shouting insults at the crowd, calling them "rabble" and "riff-raff," knocking Romantic poets aside with their nightsticks. Watch out, Shelley! Oh, he's been sorely used! Now the two poet-bobbies have got hold of Langston Hughes. They're arresting him for saying, "A poem should be simple." But if they think that this crowd of Romantics, Communist Party fellow travelers, and feminists will just part for them like the Red Sea and allow them to haul Hughes away, they are a couple of ding-dongs. *Ding-Dong*, the very words ring like a bell, to jingle-jangle me back to my task, which, as we recall, was to take an immediate political concern and to make of it something universal and timeless, more or less in the manner of Robert Lowell's "For the Union Dead," Adrienne Rich's "The Burning of Paper Instead of Children," or Walt Whitman's "When Lilacs Last in the Dooryard Bloomed."

Not too difficult an endeavor, really, since no matter what we might make of the B61-11, the ruling oligarchy of the US uses the same old divide and conquer/bread and circuses strategies of empire that the Romans used two thousand years ago. Pretty timeless, right? Nope, they're carting off Hughes for "Let America Be America Again."

Ode on a One-Armed Man

If Martin Scorsese made *Invasion of the Body Snatchers*, there'd be a better sound track than in Siegal's 1956 film. And we'd probably get the story from the point of view of a pod person—something like: "As far back as I can remember, I always wanted to be a pod. Those pseudo-people got respect. Nobody gave them parking tickets." This is what gives me the willies about Robert Lowell. It's not just that he was respected by that conservative Southern gentlemanly crowd. Scorsese would've had at least one kickass tracking shot: Becky's father pulling a pod off of the back of the truck, dragging it across the front lawn, past the 1956 Plymouth, into the kitchen, past the dog with the human face, down the stairs to the cellar, and finally planting the thing in the old family chest. But now the bulb in the fridge is blown and I can't find the tofu. You'd think with six months of refrigeration repair in my past, I could handle this sort of emergency: "He'll defrost that fridge when he comes to it," you'd say. Allen Tate was a member of the Fugitive Poets—a group of Southern white gentlemen who were proud of their heritage. You know, Klan revivals, auctions of antique lawn jockeys, male-only public fondlings of firehoses. I think there used to be some police lieutenant on their trail. Of course, the pods attacks would be much more sexual if David Cronenberg directed *The Body Snatchers*. They would perhaps rub some organic fertilizer on their victims' bodily orifices. And where the hell are my bean sprouts? It was Lieutenant Gerard who chased them, but as I remember Robert Penn Warren blamed the whole thing on carpetbaggers, scalawags, and Canadian film directors. Cronenberg would feature his obligatory neo-Hitchcockian bathtub scene in which a six-foot pod shlurches up from the drain after an unsuspecting Barbara Steele, who'd just readied herself to relax in the tub with a little John Crow Ransom. On their victims' bodily orifices, the pods would perhaps rub some orgasmic fertilizer. It's not that I mind Southern gentlemen. Why, some of our best friends and presidents were Southern gentlemen, but considering Robert Penn Warren's status and all, how can American poets finally say good-bye to the concerns of these Fugitives? One can't just say "Ciao." Or hope for a final episode when some one-armed man reveals himself. I've given up on the tofu. Adieu. Later. But I wouldn't mind coming across a mint for a julep or two. And Oliver Stone? In his version Michael Douglas would hide out in a cave with Kathleen Turner who'd fall asleep but then wake up and kick him in the balls. Bon voyage. He'd stumble forward, mumble something about the CIA, stretch out his arms, and fall, Christ-like, to the ground. But what I want to know is this: how is it that the Allen Tate who refused to meet with Langston Hughes in 1932 is in the African American poet's 1966 anthology? Does this seem like the same guy to you? Wait. I gotta stop for a minute. Now the bulb in the pantry's gone and I can't even find the miso soup. How do we say good-bye to those Fugitives? "See ya later, Allen Taters." But never mind me. I'll just be stumbling around hungry and ineffectual in the dark while Oliver Stone splices real footage of farmers planting soybeans and laborers delivering refrigerators to original sequences of pods shplurting from the ground and attacking late-nite snackers. But the very idea that all or even most Southern gentlemen are pod people—Lyndon Johnson, for instance—it not only offends the sensibilities, it gives me the Willie Carlos Williams:

This Is Just to Say

The pods
that were in
the icebox
have eaten me

and probably
left an exact
copy to join you
for breakfast

Forgive them
I was delicious
and so warm
blooded

The End-of-Days Blues

The four horsemen of the apocalypse rode in on the scent of bitter almonds. The jig was up, buddy, and it didn't take any Sterling Brown to ask the working drinking loving preaching or gambling person what they're going to do now when we see the end of the world staring us in the face like David Caruso giving the orders to a recalcitrant underling on *CSI: Miami*: "If he's not here, he must be somewhere else. Go find him." Of course, for the simile to work—and I'd not only suggest that it does, but that it should be considered a contemporary version of a Homeric-style epic simile; it *is* the apocalypse we're discussing, after all—you have to put yourself in the position of the "he" in Caruso's sentence and then think of Caruso as Satan or Old Man Death himself. Go ahead, try it. In the meanwhile, we'll ask David Cronenberg:

> Whatcha gonna do when Hollywood's on fire,
> Hollywood's burning, Mr. Disturbing Movie-Making Man?
> I'm gonna make my disturbing psychological movies
> With the gynecological instruments for mutant women,
> Gonna disturb that audience, Oh my Lord.

As you may've noticed, that apocalyptical "Left Behind" series has been doing very well on the *New York Times Book Review*'s best sellers list, I believe in fiction, though you never can tell, what with the success of James Frey with everybody and Oprah for a time, and the rise of the religious right. As I understand the premise of the series, it's more or less the end of days and Jesus comes back and carts off everyone's derrière. Since no one can sit down, they choose up sides for a stand-off between good and evil that sells sequel after sequel. Did the scent of bitter almonds just get stronger? Well, no matter how almondy the atmosphere gets, we're not putting one of those Christmas-tree shaped pine-scented air fresheners in *our* car. It's a pretty non-pretentious model, by the way. A Toyota. We can't afford much, Beverly and I, who have always much preferred *Columbo* to *CSI: Miami*. The acting's better. The mode of transportation is much less pretentious. And the special effects on *Columbo*! Remember when Robert Culp inadvertently murdered the woman he was trying to blackmail in that first-year episode? She falls into the glass table and there's her battered body on the floor and shattered glass everywhere. Then the close-up on Culp. And in either frame of his glasses the crime scene clean-up: in the right lens we see him removing her fingerprints from his room; in the left lens he's putting her body in the trunk of his car. This is the way many contemporary evangelists envision Jesus on Judgment Day, separating the good from the evil. One of Sterling Brown's points in "Memphis Blues" is, of course, that it doesn't matter a hoot to regular folk when the so-called "great civilization" suffers what it deems a catastrophe, because for most of us every day can be a catastrophe. And, you know, that's a mighty Marxist *and* Black liberationist insight. Think about how often someone is fired, their livelihood taken from them on a whim. Or laid off. And we're supposed to think it's the natural workings of an economy that these days runs in anything but free and natural fashion. Not that nature is always so kind and gentle. In "Tupelo" John Lee Hooker sings, "It rained and rained, both night and day." But I have to ask Robert Culp:

Whatcha gonna do when Columbo gets you,
Tricks you into confessing, Mister Murdering Man?
I'll be back next season to murder again,
I won't let him fool me with his, "Oh, one more thing…"
Gonna murder right next time, Oh my Lord.

Another of Professor Brown's points is that people are gonna be what they are, regardless. A very perceptive insight, and one I gotta talk over with him when I get to Heaven. I've often asked myself, for instance, "Whatcha gonna do, when the end of days comes round, / Mr. Not-Incredibly-Well-Published-Poetry-Writing Man?" Oh, except for about 144,000 people. In the "Left Behind" series, I mean. Those are the ones on account of faith and grace who have their asses saved. Kindness and humanity don't matter at all. In fact, I think the series *is* on the non-fiction best sellers list. I try to tell myself, "I'm gonna keep writing non-incredibly-well-published poetry, / Gonna keep writing it and sending it out, / Gonna keep being not incredibly well published, Oh my Lord." John Lee Hooker sings, "The poor people was worried; they had no place to go." What they thought when they were running down the stairs of the Twin Towers. What they promised their own personal God when the levees broke in New Orleans. So did you try thinking of Caruso as Satan? Or maybe he's just the pale rider out of Revelations in his pretentious Hummer. With what's being done to Christianity these days, you *do* expect the four almond-scented apocalyptic nightmare riders to come in SUVs or BMWs or Maseratis. Actually, I think the whole "Left Behind" idea was stolen from Stephen King, who, after all, authored *The Stand*. John Lee Hooker sings, "Lord have mercy, because you're the only one…we can turn to," because it does seem like the people most exploited and oppressed *do* suffer the major catastrophes of civilization more harshly, just like they do the worries everyday. Sterling Brown's nodding, explaining his use of call and response to the angels who surround him. And I'll be the son of a close-up on Caruso if I wouldn't like to number myself with Mister Preaching Man and Mister Drinking Man, with Mister Murdering Man and Mister Disturbing Movie-Making Man, but I don't know. It's difficult to hold together these apocalyptical concerns with no more than poetical duct tape, one half-assed epic simile, and a couple of O'Doul's.

The Function of the Orgasm

Without it, there would be no advertising. Imagine: America without billboards, sans signage, and no one the wiser regarding Burma Shave. There would probably be a lot fewer people in Congress. Total of three. If you surf the Web, you'll find an under-a-minute video of the guy gulping a beer and getting tazered in the ass. But why the wistful remembrance of those early suburban times when hubby arrives home after a hard day at the advertising agency, inventing every one of those innovative ways to convince the all-but-thoroughly-exploited proletariat to think of themselves as consumers so they can be further exploited? The scent of sliced-ham-and-sweet-potato TV dinners wafts up from the coffee table, and on the plastic-covered couch the wife is bedroozled out from her third martini, whereupon—hallmark of his perspicacious love!—hubby notes her navel's a shadowy pool wherein mermaids sing and Aquaman rides a seahorse. How ready for an evening of love he must be! On the TV it's *Death Valley Days*, brought to you by 20-mule-team Borax. And don't those mules look tantalizing too? The word *fuck* has many metaphorical and nonsexual meanings. It makes him, and it mars him; it sets him on, and it takes him off; it persuades him, and disheartens him; makes him stand to, and not stand to. On the bright side, we have rock: "Sunshine of Your Love," "Romeo and Juliet," "Gimme Shelter," "Layla." If you use the words *surf* and *web* in the same sentence without giving it much thought—What? Are we all California spiders?—I'm not sure you actually deserve an orgasm. Without it, the horror film never would've gotten off the ground. You know, "We have the technology," says one of the Mantle twins, but try to imagine *Dracula, The Mummy* or *The Wolfman*—criminey and crackers! especially *The Wolfman!*—without the orgasm. You know the joke: a guy sits down at the bar, orders a shot, and when it comes, a little man jumps out of his shirt pocket, gulps down the drink, then takes a running leap back where he came from. Oh, whither the baseball metaphor? First base? The home run?

> General Turgidson
>> In his boxer shorts
>>> On the phone with the base.

And the Lord said, If I find in Sodom fifty righteous within the city, then I will spare all the place for their sakes. There would be no Supreme Court. Vomiting for the purpose of sexual arousal is called *emetophilia*. What will these perverts think of next? Did I mention all the skyscrapers? Where would Aristotle be? Or Gustav Freytag? Where would be the denoument? Oh, my beautiful denoument! The word *fuck* has many rhetorical and nonsensical meanings. You can't blame someone for thinking about the musical route to the great sex life, but what do you do when your parents can't afford guitar lessons and the only tune you can pick up is "Come on Down to My Boat, Baby"? Greek mythology'd be more or less devoid of metamorphoses. Come to find out Lon Chaney's problem—the full moon, the hairy palms: not even masturbation can raise us above the animals. Imagine no advertising: this nation would have to actually *be* democratic, peace-loving and free. On the jerkoff side, there's the sociopaths: Ted Bundy, Dennis Rader, the Green River Killer, Ronald McDonald, Dick Cheney. Well, c'mon, why else shoot your friend in the face? ("Oh, my Christ! That feels good!") Why else invade Iraq (besides paranoia and oil—that *Last Tango* scene and I can't believe it's not butter)? Then, you know, guy in a bar and the same thing happens two or three times and the bartender just has to ask, so the guy tells him about finding the magic lamp and rubbing it and out comes a genii who grants only one wish. On the really bright side: "Back on the Chain Gang," "Like a Hurricane," "We Gotta Get Out of This Place," "Lola." Six of our last seven presidents would have found other occupations. In fact, it's doubtful we'd even have an executive branch of government. Balance of powers? Oh c'mon, this is your president we're talking about—"Balance this." You could have all the perversions in the world and they wouldn't be any fun. And where would be our postmodern poets and flash fiction writers who number their discrete statements so as to avoid an all-too-probable phallocentric climax? Imagine *Psycho* without it: not a toilet to be flushed on any reel. The word *fuck* has many historical and eventual meanings. He tells the bartender he wished for a nine-inch prick. Like you didn't know, my intriguing, seductive denouement. Come to find out there's a correlation between vasectomy and Primary Progressive Aphasia, a dementia that impairs word recall and the ability to understand words. See also *hump, jazz, lay,* and *screw.* Then the Lord rained upon Sodom and upon Gomorrah brimstone and fire from heaven. Washington DC would be a ghost town. Moreover, there would be no masturbation. Well, considerably less masturbation. No runs, no hits, no errors. "What do I want to transmogrify into a stupid swan for?" asks a bedreeped Zeus. All perved up and no place to go. On the incandescent side: "Thunder Road," "Don't Fear the Reaper," "Piece of My Heart," "Night in My Veins." And the end of *North By Northwest*? Leo G. Carroll rewards Eva Marie Saint and Cary Grant with a guileless, reticent smile and plane tickets home.

Just Irks Me No End

Some people work themselves into a bad mood; for others it's genetics or just, well, bad luck. My father used to move the furniture of a Saturday afternoon, trying to ascertain the perfect arrangement, growing increasingly dissatisfied, swearing, first under his breath, then with added volume and authority, until he'd give it up altogether and head out to the local tavern. This was before the heyday of feng shui, at least in the Chicagoland area. The word *mood* comes from a prehistoric Germanic word meaning "courage" or—wouldn't you know it?—"anger." Then there's seasonal mood swings—spring and summer we're fine, but about a week before Groundhog Day, it's "I HATE EVERYTHING!" Remember mood rings? Try to think of something pleasant. Genetics would suggest that bad moods run in families, skip a generation, then settle down in front of the TV with the remote and a six pack and complain about the lousy programming and we're paying forty five bucks a month for this crap? The word *bad* has quite the controversial history, derived as it is from the Anglo-Saxon *baeddel*, meaning "hermaphrodite," and *baedling*, meaning—in the biblically distempered language of yesteryear—"sodomite." And I suppose if you're in a bad enough mood, you might feel that you're driven on by flames over the barren burning plain of Hell's seventh circle, your only companion your charcoal blackened mood ring, all the while knowing if this particular bad mood lasts long enough, people come to think of you as a "bad egg" or as "bad news," suspect you of "bad-mouthing them." From herpes to rabies, a wide spectrum of viral infections can really bring you down. It's so unfair. Bruce Banner in a bad mood becomes the incredible Hulk; Clark Kent in a bad mood is the same old reporter. Ah! But Clark Kent in a phone booth! That's another story. But where do you find a phone booth these days? The Batcave? What I *do* remember is when my sister and I would become grouchy and pugilistic, my mother would tell us, "You're just tired," making, by means of her evasions of our just grievances against one another, our bad moods all the worse until exasperation finally lulled us to sleep. In Old English, *mod* could also mean "pride" and "state of mind." Speaking of pugilistic, certain Southerners are still in a snit over what they regard "the War of Northern aggression." Bunch of raggedy-old-motheaten-flag-hanging whining babies, if you ask me. *Bad egg* as a pejorative term came, of course, from the smell, which says nothing about whether it predates the expression "madder than a wet hen." Moreover, to be *in* a bad mood sounds like one is contained or surrounded—"in a bad neighborhood"—reminding us how much the term *Chicagoland area* puts me in a bad mood, being, as it is, lingo from the world of advertising, but not as bad a mood as language derived from the godforsaken corporate world: *the bottom line* or *multi-tasking*. I can feel my butt burning already. And even when our mood improves, there's still some aura about us of the courageous hermaphrodite working oneself into a lather.

All in All, a Pretty Good Day

Publishers Clearing House is at the front door with one of those humungous checks. The tune that's going around and around your head from your teenybopper days is a good one, like "The Times Are A-Changing" or "Let's Spend the Night Together." After how many years together, we wake up more in love than ever. That cheese submarine tastes orgasmic! The newspaper headline reads: "Poll shows 100% of News Reporters Correctly Distinguish *Prone* From *Supine*." We find that we can trust just about anyone over thirty. Hold the phone! That was the boss calling to say, "Take the rest of the week off." Prime-time TV runs commercial free. That toothache goes away all by itself, as did those unsightly nose hairs. And running through so many happy heads, songs like "Get Together" or "I Think We're Alone Now." The dogs take themselves for a walk. Meanwhile, winter is canceled. It was I don't know how many years ago today, the Beatles were cloned; now the band has reformed. Ditto for Traffic, the Temptations, the Grateful Dead, the Supremes, the Mothers of Invention, the Left Banke, Buffalo Springfield, the Byrds, the Four Tops, the Lovin' Spoonful, Steppenwolf, the Cryan' Shames, Herman's Hermits, the Doors, the Mamas and the Papas, the Youngbloods, the Turtles, Laura Nyro, Townes Van Zandt, and Marvin Gaye. You've lost weight haven't you? The boss calls back to say, "You'd better take the rest of the month." Magazine ads are discontinued. The border patrol stops patrolling, and world leaders decide that national borders were pretty damn silly after all. Maybe the song in our heads is

"People Got to Be Free" or "Could Be We're in Love." Suddenly, the public domain expands to include all corporate logos. The dogs feed themselves, then swoosh over, bringing us the remotes so we can watch some commercial-free TV. The in-depth newscast informs us (and quite thoroughly, I might add) that much to the bedevilment of numerous ministers, rabbis, and priests (not to mention the editors of *The Weekly World News*), Satan has never escaped from Hell. In fact, he's never even tried. He has no interest in vying for possession of human souls with whatever cosmic forces of righteousness and justice prevail in our universe—ours being one of many, by the way, each better than the one before, and we've got many universes to go. Satan just wants to play Parcheesi, eat his unbelievably orgasmic cheese sandwich, and pay attention to that Sixties tune going around in his head, "Don't Let Me Be Misunderstood." Peace on Earth. My poetry is becoming wildly popular—soon to be a major motion picture. Christopher Walken will play Satan. By the way, the doctor called and said, "You know that old saying, 'You're not getting any younger'? Well, the funny thing is, it doesn't apply anymore." While "Imagine" runs through my head, I set down the remote, needing some time to sit and take in the latest poll, which establishes that not only are Americans losing weight and discriminating between *lay* and *lie*, but also they're calling a halt to the exploitation of one human being by another. During capitalism's going-out-of-business sale, you can put in an hour or two of labor at your local multinational and receive the remuneration of a yacht. Unless you'd rather have a hot tub. Motorcycle? Mobile home? Convertible? Rocket ship? "Do You Believe in Magic?" Some seventy years ago Langston

Hughes wrote, "Let America Be America Again," and now racism, sexism and homophobia have been abolished. God really does bless us, everyone. Every time it rains, it rains manna from Heaven. Here comes the proletarian revolution! Peaceful like. Let's have another cheese sub, honey!

Gesundheit!

Philosophy is nothing to sneeze at. Friedrich Nietzsche believed we should live our lives as if allergy season were eternally recurring. Zeno supposed you could halve allergy season repeatedly and yet never get to the end. Something like how it's "Always Coca-Cola": one version of hell. Halves and halve nuts. That explains why midway through anything from academic semesters to space flights people feel the most stressed out—tenure trekkies can't squiggle semi-indecipherable comments on one more paper; astronauts worry: "We'll run out of Tang!" And in space, no one can hear you sneeze. Of Plato's ideal allergen Montaigne remained skeptical even though his eyes watered and his nose ran, yes, in the family. Everything for Spinoza following necessarily from the immutable will of God, your sneeze could have been nothing but—not cough nor burp nor hiccup. In a stunning renaissance, physics bursts from metaphysics and constructs the world as a vast and marvelous sneezorium. Occam's razor, the principle of sufficient reason: these insights cannot apply to the abstract sneeze but only to the concrete historical sneeze in its relations with the world. No sooner out of Erasmus's mouth are the words "To wipe your nose on your sleeve is boorish" than economics and aesthetics become independent areas of human endeavor and it seems a quarter— or rather an eighth—of the population can afford decorative or monogrammed handkerchiefs. Maybe a sixteenth. Some strident anti-Marxists claim that Hegel's dialectical tension between the sneezes of allergy season and those of winter colds led us straight to the February Revolution. Halfway through mortgage payments, homeowners howl, "What the swan-boppin Zeus happened to the interest rate?!!" Before John Locke advanced generalizations about life in the state of nature, he called the sneeze "nasty, brutish and short." Scot Tissue Towels asks, "Is Your Bathroom Breeding Bolsheviks?" And you should see the look on the guy's face in the 1930s ad. No way is he tempted to use these harsh towels on his nose, Erasmus' injunction notwithstanding—which injunction, by the bye, actually arrives a couple hundred years before the afore-mentioned developments in human intellectual endeavor, but it *feels* like no more time's passed than it would take to pull a hanky from your purse or the breast pocket of your suit jacket. Then there's Kant: we never know the allergen-in-itself but we sneeze all the same, a sort of meeting what plagues us halfway. And it's that halfway mark that maybe the mind can't take—the thought, "Gadzooks! I've come so far that there's no going back and I've still got just as far to go." Might be the feeling you're halving now, wishing, "Would we were that far along in the poem." In either the Greek or Roman pantheon not a single Titan or hero "abruptly sneezed retreat and reversed it to victory," even though Friedrich Nietzsche taught that when an optimist gazes for long into an abyss, he sees it as half full. Lady Philosophy instructs Boethius that happiness comes from within, but so does the wacky histamine response to myriad and sundry allergens. And the February Revolution's just around the corner from you-know-what (hint: title of an Eisenstein film [not the one with the baby carriage]), and meanwhile you're up to your nose in Mensheviks, anarchists, sealed trains, Bolsheviks, Central Committees, Provisional Governments,

Gregorian Calendars, April Theses, Kulaks, Duma deputies, more Bolsheviks, July Days, Kadets, (did I mention Soviets?), White generals, Centrists, Social-Revolutionaries, Kronstadt sailors, even more Bolsheviks. Or perhaps it's one-one-hundred-twenty-eighth of the population with the monograms. Given half a chance we'd glance back at Ancient Rome, where the apocryphal vomitoriums sit kitty-corner to the wholly mythical sneezatoriums. Then the complementary thought, "Pimples are nothing to sneeze at either, because they don't mean nothing." Please, watch those double negatives, they're aesthetically uneconomical if not just plain vulgar—Samuel Johnson refuting Bishop Berkeley by blowing his nose, showing off his snotrag (a multi-colored linen square, we'd imagine, some say worn around his head in lieu of a nightcap—not this particular kerchief, mind you, one that reminds you to pull a tissue from your conveniently placed major brand-name box of *mouchoirs blancs*, leaving us to wonder whether the heyday [or hay fever day] of the monogrammed hanky produced from alligator purse or breast pocket has all but passed, like about umpteen minutes ago). That kind of behavior spreads disease. Just ask Lucretius, a plague is nothing to sneeze at. Neither, by the way, is the development of economics as a legitimate social science, even if only one-five-hundred-twelfth of the population can afford those old-fashioned monogrammed handkerchiefs. And as for aesthetics, the tissue boxes come in soothing colors and flowery prints. But hasn't our conversation taken a turn? Turn? Turn? To everything there is a sneezin'. Lately capitalism has been sneezing its head off and half the time the invisible hand can't find it's own nose. And what *is* this pimple anyways? Pimple, my groin! That might be a bubo! It's the plague!—*O rota fortuna!*—of boils/ of lice/ of flies/ of locusts/ of frogs/ of dust mites/ of dog dander/ of ragweed pollen/ of watery eyes/ of timothy pollen/ of poplar pollen/ of sneezing cattle/ of mucus production/ of home foreclosures/ of hickory pollen/ of trickle-downs and broken levees/ of blood red rivers/ of nowhere to hide/ of dust on the curtains in the blue room/ of harsh recycled tissues/ of imported shoddy commodities made by super-exploited workers/ of sagebrush pollen/ of wasps and hornets/ of cat dander/ of crop circles/ of mugwort pollen/ of intergalactical pod pollen/ of vermin and varmint dander/ of half-baked conspiracy theories/ of cockroach protein and mold spores/ of mortgage securities bailouts/ of melamine in pet food and baby formula/ of blood-flecked sputum/ of wars and rumors of wars/ of eternally recurring recessions and depressions and we gotta get outta this place/ of darkness by day and vampires flying in the night and capital/ of half-baked conspiracies/ of nowhere to run to, nowhere, ain't got nowhere to hide/ of brightness falls from the air in phosphine glare/ of box elder pollen/ of redroot pigweed pollen/ of dust on the window casements in the green room/ of the seven deadlies gone global/ of pod persons and vampire servants in high places slavering to suspend the Constitution and get on with Armageddon/ of tumbleweed pollen/ of pollen's illimitable dominion over all/ of what?—the hail?—just as soon as you think you've got everything sort of half figured out,

The Day They Outsourced America

There are still two major political parties; it's just that now you're choosing between the Bharatiya Janata Party of India and the Chinese Communist Party. The balance of powers remains intact, although now we're balancing private contractors, domestic and foreign (some quite successful drug lords as well). Local government's more or less unaffected by these latest reforms, even if jurisdiction and staffing are now greatly reduced (three old fellows with an accordion and an armadillo watching over the banister). Newly privatized state colleges will benefit from the sale of prime real estate and relocate to more economical sites—the University of Iowa, for instance, to Whigspit, Pennsylvania—students sharing in said benefits with timelier notices of class cancellations and department closures. Most private universities will conduct online classes only—lectures and tests originating from various Free Economic Zones, pre-translated into English for student convenience. You might say it's almost ironic in a New Criticism kind of way wherein the audience is cognizant of far more than the major players on the stage of a nation initially so interested in independence and freedom. Why, you can almost hear William Empson mutter, "Of the socioeconomic situation, there's simply no type of ambiguity." One of the old gents would rather have an iguana, thank you. But these are merely the shadows of things to come, and some problems, if they don't affect us directly, we tend not to concern ourselves with them—the urinary incontinence of sheep, the heartbreak of codpiece discomfiture, the propensity for injury during episodes of Pentecostal multi-tasking (speaking in tongues while snake handling), various and sundry behind-the-scenes financial sector-government shenanigans ("Greazy fingers do God's counting in the Halls of Mammon.") or the poetical transmogrification of the joke as matter for aesthetical cogitation— whether it's just the way we're hardwired (as if we're in the world of speculative fiction) or that our society has become increasingly myopic and self-centered over the past umpteen generations. Even though we think of the codpiece as falling out of fashion in the late-16th century, it has remained popular in the leather subculture and among certain entertainers so that like Henry VIII, Ian Anderson of Jethro Tull, Gene Simmons of Kiss and Tom Jones of women's undergarments as brow-moppers are well-known for onstage codpieces. Wait! I got one! Why did the poet cross to prose? To get to the other side. Oh, you've heard that before. Another concern: the forthcoming "Theses on Anti-Poetry," which should be springing from my insomniac brain as Athena springs from the head of Morgan Freeman (whom I always thought would make a good Zeus). Of course, it doesn't aid sleep to count sheep if they're suffering urinary incontinence. For if they're excited enough to jump a fence... well, you surely follow the logic. This may be apocryphal, but the story is that members of the country-rock group Poco, formed by ex-Buffalo Springfield members Richie Furay and Jim Messina, and the blues-rock group Hot Tuna, founded by Jefferson Airplane members Jorma Kaukonen and Jack Cassidy, frequently performed onstage with no need of codpieces. It takes all kinds, I guess. According to Philip Dick, in our not-so-distant future of electric sheep and postwar radioactive ambience, all men and boys will wear lead codpieces. Imagine the discomfiture. Regarding future career opportunities, once every few years a seat or two opens on the Supreme Court. It's a good idea to begin practicing your "Constitutional originalism" speech today so that you can decide in favor of the De-emancipation Proclamation, wherein everyone making under a million a year will descend to the status of those "other persons" mentioned in Articles I, IV and V of our nation's Constitution. The demand for replicants far exceeding the supply, something had to give, and there are rumors that the source text the justices will be perusing in lieu of the aforementioned original document, aura-charged and now privately-owned (a Saudi oil prince, it is believed), is the instruction manual for Barbie's Dream Gated Community, translated into English from the Tagalog. Speaking of American dreams, sheep feed from China seems to be causing the urinary incontinence, but complaints sent to the guy with the accordion go unresolved despite the advanced tracking capabilities of tomorrow's satellite technology. One of the theses keeping me up at night begins by investigating the notion that like the codpiece, anti-poetry has a history and a heyday (or perhaps heydays) and a similar tension between functionality and decoration. Yet in the back of my mind, the seemingly opposite notion: the codpiece is mirrored in accentual syllabic poetry in English, with its Renaissance heyday and its own functional/decorative tension. Three men walk into a bar—a rabbi, a priest and a poet. Bartender looks from the men of the cloth to the versifier and says, "This has got to be a joke." No, that one didn't transmogrify very well. Speaking of your future, have you ever considered a career in law enforcement? One of America's fastest growing career opportunities, thanks to a substantial number of privatized police forces and prisons. The business of America is giving you the business. No taxation without replicants. Certes, the sweatshops will always be with you. Fast food joints too. Now you know whither goeth that prime real estate sold by your state colleges. And two or three humongous big-box stores—one where the Grand Canyon used to be. But it's mid-summer night, windows all over the neighborhood are open, and from next door you hear, "Ting tang walla walla bing bang. Ow! Jeepers and exasperation! That hurts!" And now you're in a quandary over whether you should dial 911 and what the problem might be—rattlesnake or ill-fitting codpiece? The big deal about irony is, as Cleanth Brooks would have it, "Through irony, paradox, ambiguity and other rhetorical and poetic devices of his or her art, the poet works constantly to resist any reduction of the poem to a paraphrasable core..." That's why my Minerva would be Janeane Garofalo. Wait, I got one. Kangaroo walks into a bar at the end of the world, says, "Lemme have a Canadian Club and a beer chaser." Bartender says, "We don't get too many kangaroos in here." Kangaroo says, "At these prices and it's the end of the world and no poetry being spoken, it's no wonder." Actually, William Empson said, "It is shown not as irony but as a grand overtone of melancholy," but who wants to be a downer, who recalls what in the name of Geoffrey Chaucer he was referring to anyway, and besides, what is poetry but transmogrification? Meanwhile, back in the 16th century: "Anne! What are you doing in my codpiece?" The fear in his voice. Speaking of piecework, did I mention the multitudinous openings in the pornography industry? What a business! Public area privatizers and pubic area publicizers! As if a symbol of our globalized economy itself, porn seems to find a new orifice every day. Meanwhile, somewhere more windblown a musically inclined android rattlesnake imagines she hears the wheezy lonesome sound of an accordion. Speaking of the shadows of things that might be or must be, is it dramatic irony when we know more about what's coming than we feel comfortable with? You don't need a replicant to know which way the wind blows. Okay, I got one. John Kay, lead singer for Steppenwolf: leather pants? yes; codpiece? yes or no? Meanwhile, in an Iowa Writers' Workshop in Whigspit, Pennsylvania, visiting faculty poet Dr. Osborne Obstreperowski asks the assembled MFA candidates to consider the following: "The joke first appeared during the administration of Richard Nixon. That the Nixon postage stamp was not working, wouldn't stick to envelopes. A Congressional Commission studies the problem and finds the answer: people are spitting on the wrong side of the stamp. The joke seemed to wane during the Ford and Carter administrations, but waxed like a harvest moon during the Reagan years. There were instances of the joke being told during the first Bush and Clinton presidencies, but nothing compared to the great revival of the second Bush regime, especially after Dubya prematurely declared victory in his Iraq war, with his aircraft carrier and his 'Mission Accomplished' banner, his aviator suit and his unabashedly protuberant codpiece. But how can I revive this joke for my latest poetry collection in our current political situation, what with a Chinese Communist Party president of the United States? Americans don't pay enough attention to international affairs to recognize the name or face of their current president." Is it our imagination, or is that accordion wheezing out a forlorn version of Hot Tuna's "Serpent of Dreams"? My theses would go on to wonder whether anti-poetry can be perceived as antiquated (for what device could possibly be considered anti-poetical after centuries of poetry's integration of anti-poetical devices?) or whether there aren't ways in which today's and even tomorrow's poetry must ever be to some degree discomfited. Or has accentual-syllabic poetry become a bad fit, period? Perhaps one way to phrase our question is, "Can poetry mutter?" It is here that William Empson might finally find an ambiguity, and, anyway, the candidates seem stumped: "Gosh, I don't know." "Shucks, I don't have a clue." "Somewhere Adrienne Rich says poetry requires 'imaginative transformation.' Would that idea be helpful?" "When I graduate, I'm going to be an 'other person' greeting people in the Grand Canyon Wal-Mart. What about you?" "An 'other person' in a McDonald's here in downtown Whigspit." "I know we're benefiting marvelously from our university's sale of its former location and all, but do we have to workshop by the flickering light of a fifteen watt bulb in the cloakroom of an abandoned grammar school?" Suddenly, Dr. Obstreperowski screams, "Chipmunks and crackers! That hurts!!" and falls over, having been bitten by the musically inclined android rattlesnake. "What could be more anti-poetical?" bemoans the future Wal-Mart slave just moments before the uncertainly illumined cloakroom's stampeded by incontinent electric sheep.

In Defense of Time Travel in Poetry

The first thing I'd do is rush to the rescue of Abraham Lincoln. There'd be choleric and conspiratorial John Wilkes Booth sneaking up the Ford Theater stairs and—surprise!—there I'd be with a passel of Pinkertons in no temper for any of Booth's *Sic semper.* "Okay, my good men, arrest the miscreant," I'd command in a passable variant on iambic pentameter, which I'd pretty much have to be speaking in the immediate post-Civil War period of American poetry. Except maybe around a Walt Whitman volume. And once Booth is safely tucked away in the hoosegow, I'm coaxing the Pinkertons, "C'mon, you guys, before you turn strikebreakers." Impressed by my substitutions on the iambic pentameter line, the agents follow me through time. We rescue from the scaffold old John Brown, whose body won't be moulderin' quite yet. "But if you alter the past," inquires the sf writer, "don't you also alter the present?" So there's Percy Shelley asking himself, "The unacknowledged instigators . . . no, educators. Unacknowledged negotiators of mankind?" And Spartacus, recently rescued near what was once called the Silarus River, by Pinkerton charioteers, tells Shelley, "Instigators *est bonum*; *melior est* legislators." This is where I take a break to zoom back to November 4, 1994, when I'm waiting in the rain outside the bookstore at Diversey and Clark and Beverly pulls up in her little blue Hyundai. Later this evening, we'll see *The Shawshank Redemption,* but first she swipes something off the table at the Thai restaurant announcing, "It's a booger!" and I have fallen in love and immortalized here not only our love but also time travel in poetry. Also, *The Shawshank Redemption*. Tim Robbins, Morgan Freeman. Also, documentary poetry as soon as you get a look-see at the movie ticket stubs and the restaurant receipt. They're right here somewhere. Wait! Was that the Wayback Machine that just buzzoomed by? Did I tell you about the time I brought a bunch of the stars from yesteryear to Barack Obama's Presidential Inauguration? William Powell and Myrna Loy, Humprhey Bogart and Lauren Bacall, Joan Crawford and Bette Davis, Jimmy Stewart, Cary Grant, Judy Garland, Gene Kelly, the Marx Brothers. You get the idea. So Joan asks, "Who's the grim bastard in the wheelchair?" "He was the vice-president," I answer. And Jimmy's flabbergasted, "You let Mr. Potter get that close to the White House?!! Holy Mackerel! What's left of the nation?! Is there anything left?!!" Meanwhile, Honest Abe is tidily installed in our guest bedroom, reading through Beverly's collection of books on himself, thoroughly bemused, "How am I so revered when I was oft labeled 'tyrant' and 'baboon'?" "Well, there's still quite a bit of debate about me," says Jack Kennedy, recently rescued from Dealey Plaza by a Proletarian Pinkerton motorcade—encircling the Presidential vehicle, frightening off would-be assassins, sweeping away fake Secret Service agents, securing the grassy knoll, the triple underpass, Houston and Elm streets, the Book Depository, the County Records, Criminal Courts and neighboring buildings. Next a few quick trips through the Sixties to Los Angeles, Memphis and New York, and we're more than ready to sing the song Dion made famous. Since we've discombobulated history, we'll have to add and alter a few verses and get help singing from Emmylou Harris and Marvin Gaye

(Martin, Bobby and Malcolm being a bit off-key after their near escapes; Lincoln having a naturally squeaky voice):

> Has anybody here seen my old friend Malcolm
> Can you tell me where he's gone?
> Think I see him coming back down the hill with
> Abraham, Martin and John Brown.

"Esto está muy much diversión!" exclaims Federico Garcia Lorca, recently rescued from Falange militia by anarcho-communist Pinkertons, who have also visited our putrid, free-range capitalistic future, where our own era is notorious for getting all the dystopia going with its fanatical privatizations, unending wars, criminal rulers, ruthless market speculations, toxic processed food, stupifying TV shows, ugly pornography, lousy body image, bad manners, reprehensible driving etiquette, and rude economic awakenings, all of which we quite successfully export the world over, and who've concluded (in prose, by the way, which, for concerns poetical is the future venue of expression), "This is a job for time travel in poetry!" Baruch Spinoza, recently rescued from excommunication from the 17th century Jewish community in Amsterdam, counsels the Pinkerton agents of change that any alterations they make will be as God intended all along, for God could not have intended otherwise but to otherwise intend than he apparently intended in the first place, and we're really only using *intend* in the loosest of senses here since the intentional fallacy has been known to God from the beginning, but could they please send him back to his excommunication, because in this particular case Spinoza's thinking that God is thinking as Allen Ginsberg (just now being rescued from a jail cell in Miami in 1972 where he and others [along with a younger version of yours truly] were tear-gassed and arrested outside the Republican Convention) says, "First thought, best thought" (plus, he prefers the moniker *Benedictus*). Waitaminute! Was that a Tardis just went kazooming by like a bat out of someplace where a bat might kazoom out of? Meanwhile, I'm with the Pinkertons, Spartacus, Garcia Lorca, Sam Beckett, W. E. B. DuBois, Emily and Charlotte Brontë, Mina Loy, Karl Marx and Frederick Engels, Langston Hughes, Herman Melville, Laura Nyro, Rosa Luxemburg, Walter Benjamin, Orson Welles, François Rabelais, Sterling Brown, Kenneth Fearing, Muriel Rukeyser, H. G. Wells, The Beatles, the Abraham Lincoln Brigade, the Haymarket near-martyrs, Joe Hill, Eugene Debs, Frank Zappa, Frederick Douglass, and Robert Gould Shaw and the 54th Massachusetts Regiment, and we're busting my younger self outta that Miami jail cell along with Allen Ginsberg. "But wait a minute!" the sf writer inquires, "If you rescue your younger self and bring him into the present, and God could naught but re-predetermine from all time all that was previously from all time predetermined, shouldn't you have rescued Spartacus in dactylic hexameter?" The poem screeches to a halt. No, not because of the persnickety temporal-aesthetical question. We've all decided to follow the 1968 Jimi Hendrix Experience/ Soft Machine U.S. tour—Chicago's Civic Opera House on February 25, Detroit's Masonic Temple on February 23, New York City's Hunter College on March 2. You get the idea. The Pinkertons have all the ticket stubs here somewhere. Whoa! Either the whole island is lurching to and fro in time or we are. Okay, back to saving humanity through better poetics. So here's

Percy Shelley explaining his thinking to Spartacus and the Red Pinkertons, "We poets really *are* the unacknowledged instigators, but I'm concerned with a literary intervention, a pedagogical adaptation." Spartacus is like, "*Quis?*" Shelley replies, "As long as we're under the rule of capital, I want those who make the laws to think we give two farthings." And class-conscious Pinkerton quizzes working-class-hero Pinkerton, "Did he just make mention of currency . . . or flatulence?" And everyone, including the sf writer and the recently rescued international proletariat, has a good laugh at capital's expense.

Notes

In addition to Wikipedia, various periodicals have been perused and plundered in making these poems, including *Scientific American, The Nation, The New Yorker,* and *Chicago Sun-Times.* Several poems—such as "The Function of the Orgasm," "Arse Poetica," "The Day They Outsourced America," and "So What Else Is New?"—feature found "material" (i.e. jokes). Certain rhetorical gestures may have media or otherworldly origins.

"Whither American Poetry?" Help with the invention of Caucasians and inventions of N.S. Shaler in John S. Haller, Jr., *Outcasts From Evolution: Scientific Attitudes of Racial Inferiority 1859-1900.* Assistance with Alexander Stephens' complaint from Eric Foner's *Reconstruction: America's Unfinished Revolution 1863-1877.* Lovecraft's pronunciation lesson from *More Annotated H.P. Lovecraft* edited by S.T. Joshi and Peter Cannon.

"The Function of the Orgasm" title from Wilhelm Reich's classic of the early psycho-analytic movement.

"So What Else Is New?" is for Kath.

"Making the Bride" is for Karen—we were raised on horror films. Original *Bride of Frankenstein* script information and Bela Lugosi quotation from David J. Skal's *The Monster Show: A Cultural History of Horror.*

"Tell-Tale Raccoon" is *so* for Beverly. As reported in The *Maryland Medical Journal, Science News, The New York Times* and elsewhere, Dr. R. Michael Benitez developed the theory that rabies felled Edgar Allan Poe. *The QPB Encyclopedia of Word and Phrase Origins* by Robert Hendrickson was etymologically helpful.

"Gratia, Poeta" is for Michael Anania. Sources include William Carlos William's *Spring and All,* W.L. Reeses's *Dictionary of Philosophy and Religion,* and Hazard Adam's *Critical Theory Since Plato.*

"The Fate of Humanity in Verse" refers to Seymour Hersh's "The Iran Plans" appearing in the April 17, 2006, issue of *The New Yorker*.

"The Man Who Read Marx" is for our history. Help with *praxis* from *A Dictionary of Marxist Thought*, edited by Tom Bottomore et al. Stats from Chris Hedges' *American Fascists: The Christian Right and the War on America* and the US Department of Labor.

"Just Irks Me No End" with assistance of *Dictionary of Word Origins* by John Ayto, *The QPB Encyclopedia of Word and Phrase Origins* by Robert Hendrickson, and *Wicked Words* by Hugh Rawson.

"The Day They Outsourced America" The actual William Empson quotation from *Seven Types of Ambiguity*. Cleanth Brooks quoted from *The Norton Anthology of Theory and Criticism* (Vincent B. Leitch, ed.). Adrienne Rich considers "imaginative transformation" in her essay "When We Dead Awaken: Writing as Re-Vision." The appointments of Lawrence Summers and Tim Geithner to appease Wall Street may be considered anti-inspirations for the poem.

Acknowledgments

Grateful acknowledgement is made to the editors of the following publications in which pieces first appeared.

> *Notre Dame Review* — "So What Else Is New"
> *American Letters & Commentary* — "The Fate of Humanity in Verse," "Working Like a Demon," "Gesundheit," and "The Day They Outsourced America"
> *Bluesky Review* — "*Gratia Poeta!*"
> *Oyez Review* — "Whither American Poetry"
> *Vectors: New Poetics* (edited by Robert Archambeau) — "Making the Bride"
> *Private Arts* — "Ode on a One-Armed Man"

The author alsso wishes to thank David Ray Vance and Catherine Kasper for their editorial pizzazz. Thanks to my teachers, colleagues, students, and friends for their generosity and kindness, to Michael Anania, Glynis Kinnan, Patricia Kowalik, Jennifer Barthel and Chris Gallagher, and Ida Roldán (therapist extraordinaire). To my family for their love: my mother Louise Rogaczewski, sisters Karen Couch—and family, William Couch, Laurie and Bob—and Kathy Elkins, Dean Elkins and family. And my father Frank P. Rogaczewski, who passed away in 1993.

Thanks and highest expressions of the Grateful Factor to Beverly Stewart for her love, insight, and sense of humor. Also, our most poetical dogs, Sam and Jasmine.

About the Author

Frank Rogaczewski holds a Ph.D. in Literature and Creative Writing from the University of Illinois at Chicago and teaches in the MFA Program at Roosevelt University in Chicago. He lives in Berwyn with his wife Beverly Stewart. They are at this very minute walking their dogs—Sam and Jasmine.

About the Publisher

American Letters & Commentary, Inc, is an independent not-for-profit corporation 501(c)(3). For twenty years AL&C has been dedicated to publishing a literary annual promoting innovative and "difficult" writing. We are immensely grateful to the Oppenheimer Foundation of Houston and to both the English Department and to The College of Liberal and Fine Arts at The University of Texas at San Antonio for their generous support of the journal. This volume constitutes our first forray into book publishing. The views expressed in this book are not necessarily those of UTSA, its administration, its employees, or its students, nor are they necesarrily the views of AL&C's editors, its volunteers, or its donors.

LaVergne, TN USA
18 October 2009
161271LV00003B/41/P